COME UP HIGHER

A Clarion Call for Traditional Churches

C. Orville McLeish

Come Up Higher.

Copyright © 2018 C. Orville McLeish.

All Rights Reserved.

ISBN: 978-1-949343-11-3 (paperback)

        978-1-949343-12-0 (e-book)

ILL HCP BOOK
PUBLISHING
www.hcpbookpublishing.com

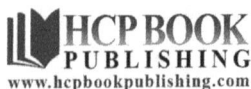

Printed in the United States of America.

TABLE OF CONTENTS

KEY TEXT

Hebrews 5:7 – 6:6 (KJV)

Who in the days of his flesh, when he had offered up prayers and supplications with strong crying and tears unto him that was able to save him from death, and was heard in that he feared;

Though he were a Son, yet learned he obedience by the things which he suffered;

And being made perfect, he became the author of eternal salvation unto all them that obey him;

Called of God an high priest after the order of Melchisedec.

Of whom we have many things to say, and hard to be uttered, seeing ye are dull of hearing.

For when for the time ye ought to be teachers, ye have need that one teach you again which be the first principles of the oracles of God, and are become such as have need of milk, and not of strong meat.

For every one that useth milk is unskilful in the word of righteousness; for he is a babe.

But strong meat belongeth to them that are of full age, even those who by reason of use have their senses exercised to discern both good and evil.

Therefore leaving the principles of the doctrine of Christ, let us go on unto perfection, not laying again the foundation of repentance from dead works, and of faith toward God,

Of the doctrine of baptisms, and of laying on of hands, and of resurrection of the dead, and of eternal judgment.

And this will we do, if God permit.

For it is impossible for those who were once enlightened, and have tasted of the heavenly gift, and were made partakers of the Holy Ghost,

And have tasted the good word of God, and the powers of the world to come,

If they shall fall away, to renew them again unto repentance; seeing they crucify to themselves the Son of God afresh, and put him to an open shame.

THE TRADITIONAL CHURCH

If you are like me, you have read the book of Acts and then looked at your church and wondered, "What happened?" Yes, Jesus established the early church, but men always had the power to change it from what it was or was meant to be. What remains true is that Jesus will build His church.

Countless articles online try to explain why the church is so different from the early church. In a nutshell, we have taught that, *"If that redemption were "completed" at the cross or on the day of Pentecost, then miraculous gifts were a useless commodity to the church."*[1] While this theology explained our experiences, I believe the cause of change goes far deeper than a divine decision that signs, wonders, and miracles were

---

1   https://www.preteristarchive.com/Hyper/0000_bell_miracles-cease.html

a part of the redemptive process and was no longer needed. What we have seen over the last few centuries are isolated individuals pursuing God for what they read in the Scriptures and walking in the same realm as the early Apostles did. Most of the results produced through these hearts after God have been met with much skepticism from the church, and while it does look like the Bible, we prefer to hang on to our belief that it should not be happening anymore, because God decided it shouldn't.

Slowly, the supernatural consciousness of a powerful kingdom reality creeps into the four walls of the church through isolated individuals who refuse to believe Christianity serves only to get individuals to repeat the sinner's prayer, get baptized, tarry for the Holy Spirit, speak in tongues initially, and then take a position in church or find a suitable seat to occupy in the congregation.

Most traditional churches serve little purpose outside the scope of what was listed in the previous paragraph. The responsibility or requirement placed on membership goes no further than that, as we are seemingly incapable of reproducing the power endued to us by the Holy Spirit. We use the name of Jesus like a lucky charm, and we use it in safe mode so nobody ever has to ask us, "Why doesn't that work?"

It is not clear when the church started to change. Some believe it happened in 70 A.D. when the temple was destroyed, as prophesied by Jesus when He walked the earth as man. I believe the church was intended to become a body of people, with you and I being God's temple—His earthly habitation, the place where He lives. But, stubbornly, we did not just build back the temple; instead, we have erected many temples we call the 'house of God,' which is biblically incorrect. However, it is safer for the world to believe their problems can be solved by coming to a 'house' for help, not to us.

True Christianity was always bred and thrived under deep persecution. Even today, real Christian loyalty is tested by the fires of persecution in various countries. These stories don't make the news though, but it is clear that a liberated form of worship produces weaker, less committed Christians.

Christianity was always an outcast community. It was Constantine who made Christianity legal, for political gain some believe. Whatever the reason, Christianity spread through his influence, but it was not the same as it was and would prove never to be the same centuries later.

The church was given a structure, became institutionalized, and tradition based. We were trapped in a cycle of doing the same thing but expecting different results. We taught that backsliders are those who stopped coming to a building and sinners should come to us to be saved, rather than us going to them. This lasted for centuries, but it was never enough for a few people who decided to break free or untether themselves from the system.

The Church Age started to end when non-church goers, filled with the Holy Spirit, begun to move in the power of the Spirit outside the building. Miracles, signs, and wonders began to break out again, much to the disapproval of the majority of the church, who met this move with much skepticism. We saw an emergence of prophets, apostles, evangelists, teachers, and pastors outside the normal structure established and permeated for centuries. The church was waking up spiritually, though only a minority.

There's a general, spiritual revolution taking place today. The new agers, occultists, obeah (voodoo) gurus are positioning themselves, offering a solution to anyone who has a need by accessing the supernatural dimension. Some are using Scriptures and the name of Jesus to do it. I don't understand the full theology behind this, but I know it's happening, all while the traditional church sits dormant, singing songs of revival, burying our dead, evangelizing the saved, utilizing the systems of the world to survive an economic crisis, and crying out for the rapture so we can escape the wrath and judgment of God on most of the human race. But what if God has a different agenda?

No one knows for sure who the writer of Hebrews is. It is assumed to be Paul because of the language. It sounds like Paul's writing, but the author is really anonymous. Any theology on the authorship of this book is assumed, but whoever wrote Hebrews had insight. They were truly enlightened and saw reality outside of time, space, and matter. In this book, we find the call to *"Come Up Higher."* It was always a call for the church. We were never meant to build ministries around signs, wonders, and miracles. We were never meant to build ministries around spiritual gifts and calling. We were never meant to build buildings to house the presence of God. We were meant to be an organism that would grow from a baby into a mature son of God, coming into union with God.

This is not an attack on traditional churches. I love my church. I believe it served its purpose by keeping people like me grounded and out of trouble, but it is an immature version of the church and definitely not the 'glorious church' that Jesus said He would present to the Father in Ephesians. That means we have some growing up to do. We are still crying out for a revival when what the church needs is a reformation.

We must not be afraid to submit ourselves to the process of maturity that God wants to bring us through. You can't go to high school and argue that your teachers are teaching you wrong, and that what they are trying to teach you wasn't what they taught you in primary school.

Revelation comes based on your level of maturity. If you make a religion or institution out of it, then you and everyone else who joins will get stuck at that level. That was never God's intention for the church.

It doesn't matter which level you are at while reading this book—there is a higher place for you, but only you can decide and embark on taking that journey. Think of Peter seeing Jesus walking on the water. Jesus told Peter to "Come." Peter could have rejected the invitation and stayed on the boat with all the others. That would have been the comfortable and rational thing to do.

You are being called to a high place, and it is an open invitation to all. The choice to accept this call and make that leap of faith, or reject it, is yours.

Part 1

COMING INTO THE KINGDOM OF GOD:

The Foundational Doctrines of Christ

INTRODUCTION

The foundational doctrine of Christ has to do with discipleship. Our present, local church definition of what it means to make disciples is not accurate. Making disciples is reproducing Christ in others, in the fullness of ministering in the power of the Holy Ghost, not by excellency of speech or wisdom, and then sending them out to reciprocate. Making disciples has nothing to do with equipping people to take up a position in church.

I believe these principles are the starting point for believers, and I found it shocking when I started to pay attention to what Hebrews was talking about here. Personally, I have never attempted to raise the dead, even after being prompted to try. I have never seen a dead person come back to life. My local church is part of an international body of believers with over 300 local churches in Jamaica, and over 30,000 members, and I have never heard anyone testify within my circles about raising the dead. Some of us preach it, some of us believe it is possible, most of us are afraid to even try. Yet, Hebrews says this is 'baby stuff.' My question is, if we haven't mastered the baby stuff, what have we mastered? What qualifies us to move up the ranks in church? What makes us a great leader? How are we able to hold senior positions in church if we haven't yet mastered the baby stuff?

This is why I lost interest in pursuing 'ministry' and a 'leadership role' because I am not qualified. When put into those positions, and anyone can move up the church ranks by knowing the right people and doing the right thing, it becomes performance-based and lacks the heart and soul of true ministry. I am not interested in performing for people, aside from drama productions, yet this is the kind of church we have built while trying to attach the label of 'spirit-led.' It begs the question, "Which spirit?"

There is a call for us to become "repairers of the breach" as prophesied by Isaiah:

Then you shall call, and the LORD will answer; you shall cry, and He will say, 'Here I am.' "If you take away the yoke from your midst, the pointing of the finger, and speaking wickedness, *If* you extend your soul to the hungry and satisfy the afflicted soul, then your light shall dawn in the darkness, and your darkness shall *be* as the noonday. The LORD will guide you continually, and satisfy your soul in drought, and strengthen your bones; you shall be like a watered garden, and like a spring of water, whose waters do not fail. Those from among you shall build the old waste places; you shall raise up the foundations of many generations; and you shall be called the Repairer of the Breach, the Restorer of Streets to dwell in. (ISAIAH 58:9-12)

The one thing that stands in the way of change is fear. Our fear of change, fear of the unknown, fear of being wrong, fear of what people think, fear of disappointments, fear of losing control, and fear of death has crippled the members of the church and forced us into a corner, reciprocating failure under a false assumption and belief that it is actually working.

Salvation is easy. Getting your foot into heaven's door is easy. Making converts and church people is easy. Growing up into the fullness of Christ; confirming or morphing into His image; maturing and coming into perfection is the work that your faith should produce.

This book is for those who know there is more; for it is in knowing we will reach out for the more, thereby becoming not just converts making converts (as is the present state of our churches), but conduits of God's magnificent, life-changing light and power.

What say you, friend? Do you just want to get your foot in heaven's door, or do you want to change the world? If the latter is your conscious choice, then read on.

P.S.

I don't know everything. I am still learning. I have a lot of knowledge I will not share in this book, because knowledge must first become experience before we can adequately attempt to articulate it. And, there are experiences in God that cannot be articulated—a place that can't be described, understood, or imparted. Jesus Christ is the door into a realm of unlimited mystery, but it can only be experienced by you personally because no one will be able to describe those experiences to you. Remember, Paul said:

> And I know such a man—whether in the body or out of the body I do not know, God knows— how he was caught up into Paradise and heard inexpressible words, which it is not lawful for a man to utter. (2 CORINTHIANS 12:3-4)

There is only one way to hear and see what Paul heard and saw in that experience, and that is to go there yourself.

So, with that said, consider this book a small doorway into the mystery that God desires to unfold in your life, and use it as a basic guide for further study, intending to be drawn by the Spirit into the experience on which this theology is based.

Chapter 1

REPENTANCE FROM DEAD WORKS

*Therefore leaving the principles of the ₁octrine of Christ, let us go on unto perfection; not laying again the foun₁ation of repentance from **dead works**, an₁ of faith towar₁ Go₁.* (HEBREWS 6:1)

The first item on the list of principles defining spiritual immaturity is Repentance from Dead Works. A lot is said or insinuated about this in Scripture. Let's look at some verses that directly quote this:

How much more shall the blood of Christ, who through the eternal Spirit offered himself without spot to God, purge your conscience from **dead works** to serve the living God? (HEBREWS 9:14)

Even so faith, if it hath not **works**, is **dead**, being alone. (JAMES 2:17)

But wilt thou know, O vain man, that faith without **works** is **dead**? (JAMES 2:20)

For as the body without the spirit is **dead**, so faith without **works** is **dead** also. (JAMES 2:26)

Dead works have to do with abiding by laws, rules, and regulations that directly affect an individual's actions but does nothing to transform the heart. We can always get people to do the right thing by enforcing rules, but their action produces no change in their intention, motive, and desires, so it is considered a dead work.

Repentance is turning away from something in order to face something else. Repentance from sin is turning away from sin to face God, who is holiness. Repentance from dead works is turning away from that which fails to produce life. This is something we must do and understand as a baby Christian, but it is not a place to erect a tabernacle of worship.

An article written by Anthony Carter says it this way:

Dead works are the works of our hands. These are works of self-righteousness, and they are appropriately called "dead" works because they lead to death. Twice the book of Proverbs says, "There is a way that seems right to a man, but its end is the way to death" (14:12; 16:25). We rely on work. We get significance from our work. We like a job that is well done. And well we should, because God created us to work. Yet all of our labors are useless, and thus dead, if they do not point to the worship of God. Any significance and esteem we attain from our labor apart from the end of bringing God glory and establishing His rule upon the earth is misplaced. Such godless labor may appear good to us and even receive the applause of others, but heaven finds it repulsive and defiled by sin. In other words, unless we have been washed in the blood of Christ, all our good deeds are worthless, useless, vain, and dead.[2]

I believe repentance from dead works also has to do with being stuck in a perpetual cycle of repentance, always dealing with something in the bloodline, generational curses, demonic oppression, sins, etc. Instead of going to the throne of God boldly, you

---

2   https://www.ligonier.org/blog/what-are-dead-works/

remain at a distance in your unworthiness, brokenness, and contriteness and always repenting. God wants more for you.

Chapter 2

FAITH TOWARD GOD

*Therefore leaving the principles of the ₁octrine of Christ, let us go on unto perfection; not laying again the foun₁ation of repentance from ₁ea₁ works, an₁ of **faith toward God.** (HEBREWS 6:1)*

The second item on our list is Faith Toward God. This is a big one because it is from this place the power of God is demonstrated on the earth through signs, wonders, and miracles. Let's quote a few passages on faith. There are plenty more:

Testifying both to the Jews, and also to the Greeks, repentance toward God, and faith toward our Lord Jesus Christ. (ACTS 20:21)

And Jesus answering saith unto them, Have **faith in God**. (MARK 11:22)

For ye are all the children of **God** by **faith in** Christ Jesus. (GALATIANS 3:26)

Jesus answered and said unto them, Verily I say unto you, If ye have **faith**, and doubt not, ye shall not only do this which is done to the fig tree, but also if ye shall say unto this mountain, Be thou removed, and be thou cast into the sea; it shall be done. (MATTHEW 21:21)

And he said unto them, Why are ye so fearful? How is it that ye have no **faith**? (MARK 4:40)

And the apostles said unto the Lord, increase our **faith**. (LUKE 17:5)

And the Lord said, If ye had **faith** as a grain of mustard seed, ye might say unto this sycamine tree, Be thou plucked up by the root, and be thou planted in the sea; and it should obey you. (LUKE 17:6)

Now **faith** is the substance of things hoped for, the evidence of things not seen. (HEBREWS 11:1)

It is hard to believe there is a dimension higher than faith when the Scriptures clearly say:

> But without faith *it is* impossible to please *Him*, for he who comes to God must believe that He is, and *that* He is a rewarder of those who diligently seek Him. (HEBREWS 11:6)

Coming into perfection/maturity repositions us in God where faith becomes unnecessary. Faith in God is only required for those who don't ascend or are not caught up (raptured). Jesus always told those whom He healed that their faith saved them. He didn't need faith because He was able to see everything the Father did and hear everything the Father said.

Faith Toward God is necessary for manifesting heaven on earth until you come into union with God.

Chapter 3

DOCTRINE OF BAPTISMS

*Of the doctrine of **baptisms**, and of laying on of hands, and of resurrection of the dead, and of eternal judgment.* (HEBREWS 6:2)

The third item on the list is the Doctrine of Baptisms. There are several types of baptisms mentioned in Scripture, so there is not just one baptism. Let's examine a few of those Scriptures:

But Jesus answered and said, Ye know not what ye ask. Are ye able to drink of the cup that I shall drink of, and to be baptized with the **baptism** that I am baptized with? They say unto him, We are able. (MATTHEW 20:22)

John did baptize in the wilderness, and preach the **baptism** of repentance for the remission of sins. (Mark 1:4)

And he came into all the country about Jordan, preaching the **baptism** of repentance for the remission of sins. (Luke 3:3)

But I have a **baptism** to be baptized with; and how am I straitened till it be accomplished! (Luke 12:50)

This man was instructed in the way of the Lord; and being fervent in the spirit, he spake and taught diligently the things of the Lord, knowing only the **baptism** of John. (Acts 18:25)

Therefore we are buried with him by **baptism** into death: that like as Christ was raised up from the dead by the glory of the Father, even so we also should walk in newness of life. (Romans 6:4)

One Lord, one faith, one **baptism**. (Ephesians 4:5)

The like figure where unto even **baptism** doth also now save us (not the putting away of the filth of the flesh, but the answer of a good conscience toward God,) by the resurrection of Jesus Christ. (1 PETER 3:21)

I indeed **baptize** you with water unto repentance. but he that cometh after me is mightier than I, whose shoes I am not worthy to bear: he shall **baptize** you with the Holy Ghost, and with fire. (MATTHEW 3:11)

And I knew him not: but he that sent me to **baptize** with water, the same said unto me, Upon whom thou shalt see the Spirit descending, and remaining on him, the same is he which **baptizeth** with the Holy Ghost. (JOHN 1:33)

If we make a list from these Scriptures, we see several different kinds of baptisms:

- Baptism of Repentance (Baptism of John)
- Baptism into Death
- One Baptism
- Baptism of Water
- Baptism of the Holy Ghost

Each of these baptisms is different and serves a different purpose. Many local churches have built a tabernacle on these principles, arguing between themselves regarding the 'right' way to baptize. The controversy surrounding these ideas has caused us to get stuck and force members to keep going around searching for the 'right' way.

We should look diligently into the matter of baptisms so we can master the principles and move on to maturity, instead of getting stuck arguing around such controversy.

Chapter 4

LAYING ON OF HANDS

Of the *octrine of baptisms, an* *of **laying** on of* ***hands**, an* *of resurrection of the* *ea* *, an* *of eternal* *ju* *gment.* (HEBREWS 6:2)

The laying on of hands is usually cited in Scripture as a precursor to a miracle. Most churches also consider it a way of doing impartations or activations. Let's look at some Scriptures that mention the laying on of hands:

And besought him greatly, saying, My little daughter lieth at the point of death: I pray thee, come and **lay** thy **hands** on her, that she may be healed; and she shall live. (MARK 5:23)

They shall take up serpents; and if they drink any deadly thing, it shall not hurt them; they shall **lay hands** on the sick, and they shall recover. (MARK 16:18)

And when Simon saw that through **laying** on of the apostles' **hands** the Holy Ghost was given, he offered them money. (ACTS 8:18)

And it came to pass, that the father of Publius **lay** sick of a fever and of a bloody flux: to whom Paul entered in, and prayed, and laid his **hands** on him, and healed him. (ACTS 28:8)

Neglect not the gift that is in thee, which was given thee by prophecy, with the **laying** on of the **hands** of the presbytery. (1 TIMOTHY 4:14)

Lay hands suddenly on no man, neither be partaker of other men's sins: keep thyself pure. (1 TIMOTHY 5:22)

The last verse quoted is the context in which I grew up in church. We claimed that we should not lay hands on any man suddenly. While this is scriptural, our application of it may have been a little off because we are told repeatedly that we will lay hands on the sick, and they will recover.

I am also aware that the laying on of hands is reserved for the clergy, or men and women of high esteem who are seen as qualified, by educational pursuit and years of 'ministry,' to administer God's power through laying on of their hands.

May I suggest an alternative thought? Do you realize that Peter preached his first sermon the day he got saved, and thousands came to the Lord? There is no reason to believe that Peter's conversion, or any of the other Disciples, took place before they were filled with the Holy Ghost. Immediately, they were all qualified to lay hands on the sick and see them get well. How can we tell born-again, Holy Ghost-filled believers they are not qualified? Paul also immediately began walking in the power of the Holy Spirit after being baptized and filled with the Holy Ghost.

Here we see the emergence of a new church culture and foundational principles that have nothing to do with the idea presented by the book of Hebrews. We have created a sub-culture by redefining what it means to be a 'baby' Christian that has elevated the real 'babies' to a place of prominence.

We should be teaching our members, new and old, that they are qualified to administer the power given to them by the infilling of the Holy Ghost. They don't need to go to a theological school first, nor do they need to hold a position in church. They just need to be taught the truth and guided accordingly. Every Holy Ghost filled believer is qualified in this regard:

> And these signs will follow those who believe: In My name they will **cast out demons**; they will **speak with new tongues**; they will **take up serpents**; and **if they drink anything deadly, it will by no means hurt them**; they will **lay hands on the sick, and they will recover**." So then, after the Lord had spoken to them, He was received up into heaven, and sat down at the right hand of God. And they went out and preached everywhere, the Lord working with *them* and confirming the word through the accompanying signs. Amen. (MARK 16:17-20)

This is the true definition of a believer, and it has nothing to do with academic excellence or years of church service.

Chapter 5

RESURRECTION OF THE DEAD

Of the ₫octrine of baptisms, an₫ of laying on of han₫s, an₫ of resurrection of the ₫ea₫, an₫ of eternal ju₫gment. (HEBREWS 6:2)

Bringing the dead to life is my favourite miracle in the Scriptures, especially knowing how most Christians are afraid to die. The fear of death haunts many of us, prompting us to make decisions without giving our faith an opportunity to produce the miracles we so desperately seek. Let's quote a few Scriptures that talk about this:

But as touching the resurrection of the dead, have ye not read that which was spoken unto you by God, saying. (MATTHEW 22:31)

And when they heard of the resurrection of the dead, some mocked: and others said, We will hear thee again of this matter. (ACTS 17:32)

But when Paul perceived that the one part were Sadducees, and the other Pharisees, he cried out in the council, Men and brethren, I am a Pharisee, the son of a Pharisee: of the hope and resurrection of the dead I am called in question. (ACTS 23:6)

And have hope toward God, which they themselves also allow, that there shall be a resurrection of the dead, both of the just and unjust. (ACTS 24:15)

Except it be for this one voice, that I cried standing among them, touching the resurrection of the dead I am called in question by you this day. (ACTS 24:21)

And declared to be the Son of God with power, according to the spirit of holiness, by the resurrection from the dead. (ROMANS 1:4)

Now if Christ be preached that he rose from the dead, how say some among you that there is no resurrection of the dead? (1 CORINTHIANS 15:21)

But if there be no resurrection of the dead, then is Christ not risen. (1 CORINTHIANS 15:13)

So also is the resurrection of the dead. It is sown in corruption; it is raised in incorruption. (1 CORINTHIANS 15:42)

If by any means I might attain unto the resurrection of the dead. (PHILIPPIANS 3:11)

Blessed be the God and Father of our Lord Jesus Christ, which according to his abundant mercy hath begotten us again unto a lively hope by the resurrection of Jesus Christ from the dead. (1 PETER 1:3)

But the rest of the dead lived not again until the thousand years were finished. This is the first resurrection. (REVELATION 20:5)

The resurrection from the dead speaks to present-day miracles as well as a future time when the "dead in Christ shall be raised up." What is remarkable is that Jesus alludes to the concept of death and life in a different sense that I rarely hear the church speak about:

> Jesus said to her, "I am the resurrection and the life. He who believes in Me, though he may die, he shall live. And whoever lives and believes in Me shall never die. Do you believe this?" (JOHN 11:25-26)

The church has become a place that buries the dead instead of giving life. We speak of life only after death, without ever mentioning the life that overrides death. Jesus mentioned it. Paul spoke about it when he said:

> Behold, I tell you a mystery: We shall not all sleep, but we shall all be changed. (1 CORINTHIANS 15:51)

We have not yet begun to believe and teach Scripture as our rule of faith. We carry within us the resurrection power that has dominion over death. God is love. God lives inside us. We become love, and love is stronger than death.

Chapter 6

ETERNAL JUDGMENT

Of the doctrine of baptisms, and of laying on of hands, and of resurrection of the dead, and of eternal judgment. (HEBREWS 6:2)

Eternal judgment is real but can be averted. We have used this as our sales pitch to get people saved, even more than we have used the love, mercy, and grace of God. Let's look at some Scriptures that speak about judgment:

And the angels which kept not their first estate, but left their own habitation, he hath reserved in everlasting chains under darkness unto the judgment of the great day. (JUDE 6)

But I say unto you, That whosoever is angry with his brother without a cause shall be in danger of the judgment: and whosoever shall say to his brother, Raca, shall be in danger of the council: but whosoever shall say, Thou fool, shall be in danger of hell fire. (MATTHEW 5:22)

But I say unto you, That it shall be more tolerable for the land of Sodom in the day of judgment, than for thee. (MATTHEW 11:24)

A bruised reed shall he not break, and smoking flax shall he not quench, till he send forth judgment unto victory. (MATTHEW 12:20)

But I say unto you, That every idle word that men shall speak, they shall give account thereof in the day of judgment. (MATTHEW 12:36)

For the Father judgeth no man, but hath committed all judgment unto the Son. (JOHN 5:22)

And hath given him authority to execute judgment also, because he is the Son of man. (JOHN 5:27)

And Jesus said, For judgment I am come into this world, that they which see not might see; and that they which see might be made blind. (JOHN 9:39)

Now is the judgment of this world: now shall the prince of this world be cast out. (JOHN 12:31)

And when he is come, he will reprove the world of sin, and of righteousness, and of judgment. (JOHN 16:8)

But why dost thou judge thy brother? or why dost thou set at nought thy brother? for we shall all stand before the judgment seat of Christ. (ROMANS 14:10)

For we must all appear before the judgment seat of Christ; that every one may receive the things done in his body, according to that he hath done, whether it be good or bad. (2 CORINTHIANS 5:10)

And as it is appointed unto men once to die, but after this the judgment. (HEBREWS 9:27)

For the time is come that judgment must begin at the house of God: and if it first begin at us, what shall the end be of them that obey not the gospel of God? (1 PETER 4:17)

Herein is our love made perfect, that we may have boldness in the day of judgment: because as he is, so are we in this world. (1 JOHN 4:17)

To execute judgment upon all, and to convince all that are ungodly among them of all their ungodly deeds which they have ungodly committed, and of all their hard speeches which ungodly sinners have spoken against him. (JUDE 15)

Saying with a loud voice, Fear God, and give glory to him; for the hour of his judgment is come: and worship him that made heaven, and earth, and the sea, and the fountains of waters. (REVELATION 14:7)

Standing afar off for the fear of her torment, saying, Alas, alas that great city Babylon, that mighty city! for in one hour is thy judgment come. (REVELATION 18:10)

And I saw thrones, and they sat upon them, and judgment was given unto them: and I saw the souls of them that were beheaded for the witness of Jesus, and for the word of God, and which had not worshipped the beast, neither his image, neither had received his mark upon their foreheads, or in their hands; and they lived and reigned with Christ a thousand years. (REVELATION 20:4)

There is something stronger than judgment, and that is mercy. Righteousness demands a balance between the two because that is how the Father functions, and He will always choose mercy over judgment. We see this repeatedly with the Children of Israel and throughout biblical history.

On several occasions, God pronounces a judgment on several individuals and nations. He subsequently relents from carrying it out for one of two reasons:

1. Somebody stands up to Him, most times at the risk of their own lives.

2. The individual or nation repents before the Lord.

If God can turn away from something He has already declared, then I believe we should put greater emphasis on the pursuit of mercy, love, and true intercession.

Part 2

COMING INTO
MANIFESTED SONSHIP:

The Coming Age
of Perfection

INTRODUCTION

The Book of Hebrews is multi-dimensional. It speaks to separate dimensions and levels in order to:

1. Know where we are in our personal journey with God.

2. Know where God intends to take us.

Let's read several translations for Hebrews 6:1:

Therefore let us move beyond the elementary teachings about Christ and be taken forward to maturity, not laying again the foundation of repentance from acts that lead to death, and of faith in God. (NIV)

So let us stop going over the basic teachings about Christ again and again. Let us go on instead and become mature in our understanding. Surely we don't need to start again with the fundamental importance of repenting from evil deeds and placing our faith in God. (NLT)

Therefore let us leave the elementary doctrine of Christ and go on to maturity, not laying again a foundation of repentance from dead works and of faith toward God. (ESV)

Therefore, having left the beginning teaching of the Christ, we should go on to maturity, not laying again a foundation of repentance from dead works, and faith in God. (BLB)

Therefore leaving the elementary teaching about the Christ, let us press on to maturity, not laying again a foundation of repentance from dead works and of faith toward God. (NASB)

We must try to become mature and start thinking about more than just the basic things we were taught about Christ. We shouldn't need to keep talking about why we ought to turn from deeds that bring death and why we ought to have faith in God. (CEV)

Therefore, leaving behind the elementary teachings about the Messiah, let us continue to be carried along to maturity, not laying again a foundation of repentance from dead actions, faith toward God. (ISV)

With this in mind, we should stop going over the elementary truths about Christ and move on to topics for more mature people. We shouldn't repeat the basics about turning away from the useless things we did and the basics about faith in God. (GWT)

In Part I of this book, we briefly touched on the principles of becoming a believer. There is plenty of room for you to do your own research, learn, and master these principles before you are qualified to step beyond them. You will agree with me that most of the church has no idea what the writer of Hebrews is talking about here. This is what we should be teaching new converts:

1. Repentance from dead works

2. Faith in God

3. Doctrine of baptisms

4. Laying on of hands

5. Resurrection from the dead

6. Eternal judgment

According to the author of Hebrews, this is basic Christianity. Those who master this level become disciples. That is what Jesus meant when He said:

> Go therefore and make disciples of all the nations, baptizing them in the name of the Father and of the Son and of the Holy Spirit (MATTHEW 28:19).

In essence, this is an introduction to Christianity. What we have been doing instead is making Church People. No Scripture in the Bible tells us to go and make church people, go and plant churches, or even go and build churches.

As a matter of fact, Jesus says, "I will build my church...and the gates of hell will not prevail against it" (MATTHEW 16:18). Then He says to us, "Go make disciples" (MATTHEW 28:19-20).

Once we master this basic level of Christianity, adding to this "praying always with all supplication and prayer" (EPHESIANS 6:18), we become qualified to move into a higher dimension called "coming into perfection" or "manifested sonship." We get to participate in divinity at the same level as Jesus Christ, as co-heirs, co-laborers, co-inheritors.

So, what does it look like to become mature? What is hard meat? This is a completely different dimension, untapped and unexplored by most Christians today.

We can pull a listing from Hebrews 6:4:6:

1. Once enlightened

2. Tasted of the heavenly gift

3. Partakers of the Holy Ghost

4. Tasted the good word of God

5. Powers of the world to come

This dimension is referred to as coming into maturity or perfection. I believe this is the level that Romans 8:22 speaks about when it says, "All creation is groaning and waiting for the manifestation of the sons of God."

The problem is, we take all of this and put it after our death, when in reality, this became a reality after Christ's death, and we died with Him. That's what Paul says.

Now if we died with Christ, we believe that we will also live with him. For we know that since Christ was raised from the dead, he cannot die again; death no longer has mastery over him.

The death he died, he died to sin once for all; but the life he lives, he lives to God. (ROMANS 6:8)

We died with Him. We were raised with Him. We ascended with Him and are now seated in heavenly places with Christ. This is not sometime in the future—this is now!

What bothers me is that most of the church seems to be stuck operating in a dimension lower than the basic principles of Christianity.

Yet, we have the fullness of the Godhead living inside us. Jesus said, "the Kingdom of God is within you" (LUKE 17:21).

So, my question to God has been, how can we have all this potential but can't activate it or walk in it?

I want to dedicate a chapter to each of these five principles, quoting any Scripture I can find, but I know that this dimension is beyond articulation. I can just tell you it's possible based on the experiences of others, for I am also on the journey to "Come Up Higher."

I think a great start is to know that these dimensions exist, and we can walk in them because God is no respecter of persons. If you can keep an open mind, then all things become possible for you.

Chapter 1

ONCE ENLIGHTENED

*For it is impossible for those who were once enlightened,
and have tasted of the heavenly gift, and were made
partakers of the Holy Ghost.* (HEBREWS 6:4)

Church folks fear the word 'enlightened.' We say
it's a new age word. Yet it is repeated several times in
Scripture. Here are a few examples:

To bring back his soul from the pit, to be
enlightened with the light of the living.
(JOB 33:30)

His lightning enlightened the world: the earth
saw, and trembled. (PSALM 97:4)

The eyes of your understanding being enlightened; that ye may know what is the hope of his calling, and what the riches of the glory of his inheritance in the saints. (EPHESIANS 1:18)

Enlightened is defined as "having or showing a rational, modern, and well-informed outlook." It has a lot to do with how we perceive reality.

For most of the known world, people, in general, are ignorant to life outside of the physical realm. It's hard to fathom a spiritual reality, with angels, heavens, demons, God, Jesus, the Holy Spirit, etc. This kind of outlook on life also contributes to our inability to see life outside of death. For many, death is the end of it all, so they attempt to live a full life, accomplish what they can, store up what they can, and have a lot of fun.

Christianity introduces us to a new outlook on life. There we begin to consider the eternal value of our souls, though we can't fully grasp what our soul and spirit look like, and how it should function. But there is yet a deeper experience embedded in human consciousness (another word we don't like).

The word 'fallen' as attributed to what took place in the Garden of Eden has a lot to do with consciousness as well. We lost our awareness as human beings of the Source and Reality of the

One who created us in the first place. We became unconscious of our spiritual reality.

As we walk through the foundational principles of Christianity and develop good spiritual practices, engaging God in worship, prayer, and fellowship, a new door opens that can only be described as 'enlightenment.' Paul refers to it in Ephesians 1:18 as "the eyes of our understanding being enlightened." This is the realm of mystery, where we learn the fullness of who we are as human beings and just how much responsibility and influence we have in the created world. This is also the beginning of a dimension you have to experience for yourself, because it must flow from your personal relationship with God cultivated over time by constantly engaging the unseen realm.

Chapter 2

TASTED OF THE HEAVENLY GIFT

*For it is impossible for those who were once enlightened,
and have tasted of the heavenly gift, and were made
partakers of the Holy Ghost.* (HEBREWS 6:4)

The greatest gift humanity has ever received is God
Himself. It is the mystery of all ages, how the Creator
of humanity would choose to sacrifice Himself to save
a fallen race, people who willfully disobeyed Him and
plunged an entire race into sin and lawlessness.

In the beginning was the Word, and the Word
was with God, and the Word was God. He was
in the beginning with God. All things were
made through Him, and without Him nothing

was made that was made. In Him was life, and the life was the light of men. And the light shines in the darkness, and the darkness did not comprehend it. (JOHN 1:1-5)

God inserted himself into human flesh and became one of us. He walked among us, loved us, and was rejected and killed by us. Why would God subject Himself to such torment for man? What does He see in us? What value do we really have that He would subject His divinity to fallen human consciousness?

He has not just given Himself to humanity as a gift, but He opened Himself up so that we can participate in His divinity. He became sin, so we can become righteous. He became poor, so we can be rich. He died, so we can live.

Chapter 3

PARTAKERS OF THE HOLY GHOST

*For it is impossible for those who were once enlightened,
and have tasted of the heavenly gift, and were made
partakers of the Holy Ghost.* (HEBREWS 6:4)

The ones who taste of the heavenly gift, become
partakers of the Holy Ghost. I like the use of the word
'partakers' because it suggests that we are called to be
participants in whatever God is doing. It denotes taking
an active role in whatever the Holy Ghost is doing. Let's
look at a few Scriptures that use the word 'partake':

For we being many are one bread, and one
body: for we are all partakers of that one bread.
(1 CORINTHIANS 10:21)

Ye cannot drink the cup of the Lord, and the cup of devils: ye cannot be partakers of the Lord's table, and of the table of devils. (1 CORINTHIANS 10:21)

Even as it is meet for me to think this of you all, because I have you in my heart; inasmuch as both in my bonds, and in the defense and confirmation of the gospel, ye all are partakers of my grace. (PHILIPPIANS 1:7)

Giving thanks unto the Father, which hath made us meet to be partakers of the inheritance of the saints in light. (COLOSSIANS 1:12)

Wherefore, holy brethren, partakers of the heavenly calling, consider the Apostle and High Priest of our profession, Christ Jesus. (HEBREWS 3:1)

For we are made partakers of Christ, if we hold the beginning of our confidence stedfast unto the end. (HEBREWS 3:14)

Whereby are given unto us exceeding great and precious promises: that by these ye might be partakers of the divine nature, having escaped the corruption that is in the world through lust. (2 PETER 1:4)

To partake of something is to participate or share in the fullness of that thing. Those who are partakers of the Holy Ghost share in His divine power from a realm outside of time, space, and matter, from the realm of infinity. It is as if God deliberately chose to share Himself with us by joining Himself to us.

The same Holy Spirit that hovered over the waters in the beginning and brought order and beauty from chaos embodies us and gives us access to the fullness of the Godhead in form, function, and power.

I like Moses. I believe he is a good example of walking in this realm. Let's look at one Scripture:

And the Lord said to Moses, "Why do you cry to Me? Tell the children of Israel to go forward. But lift up your rod, and stretch out your hand over the sea and divide it. And the children of Israel shall go on dry ground through the midst of the sea." (EXODUS 14:15-16)

Who parted the Red Sea? God told Moses to do it. The power to part the Red Sea was inside Moses. So, God says to us "heal the sick, raise the dead, cast out demons" in a similar way that God says to Moses "raise your staff over the sea and divide it." In terms of expressing our language, we are going to say it is the Lord who does the healing, casting out demons, raising the dead, right? But in reality, God says, you do it. I live in you, so that empowers you to do the impossible. Why do we always take ourselves, and our God-given ability to do anything out of the picture? I know you are going to quote Jesus' words, "Of myself, I can do nothing" (John 5:30), and it is true, but the whole idea of God filling a human being, suggest that we have become something different and are now able to do what God does. We must be mindful of the fact that it was always God's idea to make us who we are. We didn't have a say in the matter.

There's a realm of power that most of us are not yet matured enough to walk in. In that realm, the demarcation line of separation is completely removed. There is no difference between what we do and what the Father is doing. A cohesion of divinity is superimposed over humanity to cause a mere man to move in tandem with God. Not that we are mere men.

So, now we understand Jesus' statement when He said:

"Most assuredly, I say to you, the Son can do nothing of Himself, but what He sees the Father do; for whatever He does, the Son also does in like manner." (JOHN 5:19)

It is in this realm that this oneness becomes possible, and it is also in this realm that the true backsliding can occur that no one can restore you from. For if you get to this place, and turn away from God, it is impossible to restore you again.

P.S.

The concept of backsliding that we use in church today is not scriptural. Backsliding has nothing to do with church attendance, a position in church, or even the fact that one stops believing. Anyone who falls into these categories can easily be restored. The one who truly backslides cannot be restored.

Chapter 4

TASTED THE GOOD WORD OF GOD

I believe the Bible records the experiences of all the men and women of God to inform us that we too can have similar experiences. It is good to read the Bible; good to believe what it says; good to practice keeping the commandments, but there is still something deeper. Jesus is the Word of God made flesh. The Word of God is Spirit and it is Life (See JOHN 6:63-70). It is a living, breathing entity that pulls our spirit man into a grand experience that is out of this world. You can literally step into the Word of God. It is food and drink—a sustaining principle. Let's look at some Scriptures that alludes to the Word of God having a life of its own:

And as they were going down to the end of the city, Samuel said to Saul, Bid the servant pass on before us, (and he passed on), but stand thou still a while, that I may shew thee the word of God. (1 SAMUEL 9:27)

And it came to pass the same night, that the word of God came to Nathan, saying. (1 CHRONICLES 17:3)

Every word of God is pure: he is a shield unto them that put their trust in him. (PROVERBS 30:5)

Making the word of God of none effect through your tradition, which ye have delivered: and many such like things do ye. (MARK 7:13)

And Jesus answered him, saying, It is written, That man shall not live by bread alone, but by every word of God. (LUKE 4:4)

Now the parable is this: The seed is the word of God. (LUKE 8:11)

If he called them gods, unto whom the word of God came, and the Scripture cannot be broken. (JOHN 10:35)

And the word of God increased; and the number of the disciples multiplied in Jerusalem greatly; and a great company of the priests were obedient to the faith. (ACTS 6:7)

But the word of God grew and multiplied. (ACTS 12:24)

So mightily grew the word of God and prevailed. (ACTS 19:20)

So then faith cometh by hearing, and hearing by the word of God. (ROMANS 10:17)

What? Came the word of God out from you? Or came it unto you only? (1 CORINTHIANS 14:36)

For we are not as many, which corrupt the word of God: but as of sincerity, but as of God, in the sight of God speak we in Christ. (2 CORINTHIANS 2:17)

But have renounced the hidden things of dishonesty, not walking in craftiness, nor handling the word of God deceitfully; but by manifestation of the truth commending ourselves to every man's conscience in the sight of God. (2 CORINTHIANS 4:2)

And take the helmet of salvation, and the sword of the Spirit, which is the word of God. (EPHESIANS 6:17)

For it is sanctified by the word of God and prayer. (1 TIMOTHY 4:5)

To be discreet, chaste, keepers at home, good, obedient to their own husbands, that the word of God be not blasphemed. (TITUS 2:5)

For the word of God is quick, and powerful, and sharper than any two-edged sword, piercing even to the dividing asunder of soul and spirit, and of the joints and marrow, and is a discerner of the thoughts and intents of the heart. (HEBREWS 4:12)

And have tasted the good word of God, and the powers of the world to come. (HEBREWS 6:5)

Through faith we understand that the worlds were framed by the word of God, so that things which are seen were not made of things which do appear. (HEBREWS 11:3)

Being born again, not of corruptible seed, but of incorruptible, by the word of God, which liveth and abideth for ever. (1 PETER 1:23)

For this they willingly are ignorant of, that by the word of God the heavens were of old, and the earth standing out of the water and in the water. (2 PETER 3:5)

I have written unto you, fathers, because ye have known him that is from the beginning. I have written unto you, young men, because ye are strong, and the word of God abideth in you, and ye have overcome the wicked one. (1 JOHN 2:14)

Who bare record of the word of God, and of the testimony of Jesus Christ, and of all things that he saw. (REVELATION 1:2)

And he was clothed with a vesture dipped in blood: and his name is called The Word of God. (REVELATION 19:13)

In the beginning was the Word, and the Word was with God, and the Word was God. (JOHN 1:1)

On occasion, we see the Word of God coming to someone. The Word of God is tangible and can be seen. In Proverbs 30:5, the Word of God is referred to as a "he." The Word of God is also referred to as a seed, which means it can produce something.

We quote this saying all the time, "Come taste and see that the Lord (Word of God) is good." We usually interpret Scriptures we don't fully understand symbolically. The Bible never tells us to interpret Scripture literally, or symbolically, so it's just a personal choice. We have built many platforms and ministries on personal choice, but the invitation is open to all—eat the Word of God and live an abundant life.

Chapter 5

POWERS OF THE WORLD TO COME

And have tasted the good word of God, and the powers of the world to come. (HEBREWS 6:5)

There's not much I can say about this, except to repeat the words of Paul: "Eye has not seen, nor ear heard, nor have entered into the heart of man, the things which God has prepared for those who love Him" (1 Corinthians 2:9).

If the God of the universe really does live inside the believer, then common interpretative deduction leads me to conclude that we have access to unlimited power, even if it is only present in a state of potential. The world to come is the world that existed before time. So, the end is still the beginning.

Let's read a few Scriptures that speak of a world
to come:

> And whosoever speaketh a word against the Son
> of man, it shall be forgiven him: but whosoever
> speaketh against the Holy Ghost, it shall not be
> forgiven him, neither in this world, neither in
> the world to come. (MATTHEW 12:32)

> But he shall receive an hundredfold now in
> this time, houses, and brethren, and sisters,
> and mothers, and children, and lands, with
> persecutions; and in the world to come eternal
> life. (MARK 10:30)

> Who shall not receive manifold more in this
> present time, and in the world to come life
> everlasting. (LUKE 18:30)

> For unto the angels hath he not put in subjection the
> world to come, whereof we speak. (HEBREWS 2:5)

> Out of Zion, the perfection of beauty, God hath
> shined. (PSALM 50:2)

Here is a mystery for you: if it is in your future, you
can participate in it now. The coming age is the age
of perfection. You can participate in the coming age of
perfection now.

Part 3

TRAVERSING
BETWEEN
DIMENSIONS

INTRODUCTION

There are two things I want to look at in this final section, and that is:

- Suffering

- The heart

It is vital that we understand the role that each of these plays in moving from one dimension to the next. It's never automatic, and it doesn't come fully after death either.

You will be taught how to be a son. If not in this life, you will definitely be taught in the next. If you spend your entire life resisting the process, you will pick up right where you left off after you die, if you die.

Remember, the goal of salvation is restoration, where man is once again conformed to the image and likeness of God. Then, and only then, can we once again assume our rightful place in creation, taking up rule and dominion over the earth. Our mandate has not changed; it's just waiting for its culmination and fulfillment.

So, let's talk about suffering and the heart.

Chapter 1

SUFFERING

One of the greatest experiences to shift us between dimensions is suffering. Evangelist Valentine Rodney once said, "Those who walk in an anointing have paid the price." My mentor says, "There is no anointing without suffering." We use the term "anointing" loosely in church because most of us are not willing to pay the price to increase the anointing in our lives. The greater the suffering, difficulties faced, and tribulation, the greater the anointing.

Through suffering, we become more than conquerors because it always pushes us to a higher place. So, if you have been praying for an anointing, you have been asking for suffering.

It is the principle of the refining fire, the process that purifies, that makes gold. Your whole Christian life pulls you through that process. You are going through it right now.

Proverbs 17:3 says, "The fining pot is for silver, and the furnace for gold, but the Lord trieth the hearts."

So God gives you a difficult job, with difficult people. He did that deliberately, so stop praying for Him to give you another job.

You can't rule and take dominion of this earth until you learn to respond to difficult people with a godly heart.

David is a prime example. He went through things we only have nightmares about, but it was all a refining process because, at the end of the day, God could say, "Now here is a man after my own heart" (See 1 Samuel 13:14 & Acts 13:22).

Remember, God gave Satan permission to afflict Job. So the beef you think you have with the devil is misplaced. The One you really have a problem with is God, because nothing happens in your life without His permission.

Facing Difficulties

I have had some difficult clients in my career as a ghostwriter and self-publisher. When you get to this place, you learn not to follow and trust your heart. Proverbs 23:7 says, "As a man thinketh in his heart, so is he." I realized that God kept putting difficult people in my path until I learned to respond to them correctly in my heart. Now I get some of the nicest clients in the world.

You will never shift dimensions until you learn the lesson of the heart embedded in your experiences, and God will leave you in a cycle of going through the same thing until you do.

So, I won't tell you that God wants to deliver you from your problems. I can tell you that the quicker you learn from it, the quicker your problem will go away. If your prayer is always, "God take this away," you will find that those prayers are not always answered.

Paul had great out-of-body experiences and saw and heard things he was not permitted to reveal. To keep Paul humble, so he wouldn't exalt himself or think of himself more highly than he ought, God gave him a thorn in the flesh. Paul says, "Three times I sought the Lord to remove it, and God said no." Eventually, God said, "My grace is sufficient, for my strength is made perfect in your weakness" (See 2 Corinthians 12:8-10). We need to stop telling people to be strong when they are going through difficulties, because, in essence, we are saying God will not come through for them, so they need to figure it out on their own. What we need to say is "Be weak." God's strength is only perfected in your weakness, not your strength.

So, it doesn't matter where you are in your spiritual journey—there is a higher place. God is calling us to "Come up Higher." There are two ways to do this:

1. We learn from our experiences. The trials and difficulties we face become our teacher. It is through many trials that we come into the kingdom (See Acts 14:22).

2. We learn from those who are walking in a higher realm than we are. We must expose ourselves to teachers walking in these realms, even though initially we may be uncomfortable with the content of their message.

I believe we underestimate and devalue the purpose and necessity for teachers in the kingdom of God. We go to school to learn from people who know more than we do. Unless we are taught at a higher level than where we are, we don't move from grade to grade. Yet, we come to church and just want to hear what we already know. A teacher is supposed to know more than you do or you are wasting your time.

But rejoice, inasmuch as ye are partakers of Christ's sufferings; that, when his glory shall be revealed, ye may be glad also with exceeding joy. (1 PETER 4:13)

Chapter 2

A MATTER OF THE HEART

Most of the issues we struggle with have to do with the heart. The Bible says out of the heart flows the issues of life. The heart carries great value in our Christian journey because it sits at the foundation of every choice and influences just how much we are changed or transformed.

My entire Christian journey has now become a journey of my heart. Man looks at the outward appearance, but God sees the heart.

The **heart is** deceitful above all things, and **desperately wicked:** who can know it? (JEREMIAH 17:9)

One of the worst things you can do is to follow your heart, because the Bible says it is deceitful.

So, it says in Hebrews 5:8, that even though Jesus was the Son, He had to learn obedience through the things He suffered (things He endured, what He put up with), which suggests the experiences we go through are a test of our hearts, because learning obedience is a heart thing.

I realize that moving between dimensions is a heart issue, because if God unlocks all this power within us before we are ready, we could destroy the world if our heart is not transformed.

Out of the abundance of the heart, the mouth speaks. (See LUKE 6:45)

Guard your hearts, because out of it flows the issues of life. (See PROVERBS 4:23)

Life and death is in the power of your tongue. (See PROVERBS 18:21)

So, within our heart is the potential for both life and death, and most of us have not yet learned the language of life. We speak death, we condemn, we backbite, we gossip, we hate, we have malice, we are arrogant, and God consistently, every single day, is testing our hearts through the experiences He allows.

Chapter 3

THE CLARION CALL

There is so much potential sitting inside every believer, yet we live defeated lives because we expel so much effort fighting the process, and not giving into it. We don't expose ourselves to people who can actually teach us to move. We pray for more, and we can't see when God puts it in front of us, because of skepticism and fear. We block or reject God's answer to our prayers. We miss opportunities to grow, and, thereby, we get stuck and become elders or 'matured' in a lower dimension. In that lower dimension, you have little to offer to the world. You are just waiting to die to go to heaven. If that's what you want, God is fine with it. I am fine with it. But if you know the call of God on your life requires you to come up higher, then you must break free from this mold.

It is my prayer that this book, though brief in content, challenges us to seek God at a deeper level, and learn to see Him when He actually appears to us via teachers, and through our circumstances, for, "All things work together for good, to them that love the Lord" (Romans 8:28). So, you have all the reasons in the world to "Bless the Lord at all times, and let His praise remain continually on your lips" (See Psalm 34:1)

I will speak first to the regular churchgoer:

There are many reasons you gave your heart to Jesus and got baptized. Maybe you saw it as a solution to your immediate problems, or it just felt like the right thing to do. I want you to know there is more for you. What you are seeking, you may not find in church. The purpose of church is fellowship, not necessarily to remedy your problem. You need to start developing a relationship with God. Speak to Him as a friend, and He will respond to you. Your life should flow from that place. God wants to have a relationship with you, so start cultivating that relationship. It will become real. He wants to infuse Himself with you and become one with you. So cultivate and grow your relationship, and you will find yourself moving and growing, as God will cause you to shift in every area of your life – emotionally, economically, etc.

Second, to those who hold positions in church:

While you work and work diligently, realize that your work is not your salvation. No matter how much work you do, and the sacrifices you make, it cannot compensate for the blood of Jesus. So while you work, ensure you don't neglect what is important, which is a relationship with God. Spend time with God. Start cultivating a closer walk and relationship with God, even if you have to cut down some of the church work you do. Church work will not be rewarded. What will be rewarded is the labor that flows from your relationship with God.

Cultivate your relationship through worship, prayer, and fellowship. You don't want your spiritual practices to become mechanical. You don't want prayer and worship to become a chore, because then it will not be productive. If your prayer life is a chore because you do it the same time every day, then stop doing it the same time every day. Do it randomly and as often as you can. Do it while driving, using the bathroom, doing your chores, etc. If prayer is just a chore that you want to get out of the way, it will not produce anything. If that defines your prayer life, change it radically. Wait for the spirit of prayer to descend on you, and pray at that time, so your emotions, thoughts, and imagination are involved. Spending time with God should take priority over church work.

Third, I speak to my fellow Bible teachers:

Repetition of Scripture is not teaching. Asking your students what they think a Scripture means is not teaching. If that is your method of teaching, you may need to step away for a while. Step back a little and spend time in study. But don't just study—ask the Father to help you live what you study; to experience what you study. Teach from that place.

Teachers are held more accountable, and in a higher regard, so you don't want to mess around in this area. Teachers are very important in the kingdom of God in this day and age. If you have a gift for teaching, don't take it lightly. You want to develop and cultivate a more authoritative approach to teaching the Word of God. You want to understand what you are teaching. You want to know and experience what you are teaching. You want to grow in that area. Don't be afraid to admit that you were wrong. You can get a revelation today and it changes tomorrow. It doesn't mean your previous revelation was wrong. God will give revelation based on your level of maturity, so it can change. You will find an overriding principle taking place. Be open to it.

The purpose of teaching is to challenge people's mind. You want them to learn, think differently, and get a practical approach to their walk in Christ so they can apply principles and experience transformation. God is depending on you as an educator in the kingdom, so don't take this calling lightly. The church is where it is today because we have failed miserably in this area.

Finally, to all pastors:

You are the acting shepherd of the house. Jesus is the Shepherd and head of the church. Don't assume that position. Your responsibility is great. You are responsible for the people in your church. One thing we do wrong is put great emphasis on the wrong thing. One thing you want to be mindful of is that a proper biblical foundation is established. We see this in Hebrews and briefly discuss each point in Part I of this book. Don't lay a foundation based on church doctrine. Some church doctrines don't fit into the basic principles of Christianity. We need to de-emphasize these. Put greater emphasis on what is important.

I know numbers are important for us. But we are not supposed to be training people to keep them inside a building. We need to train them to send them out, so they can impact the world. We need to train people and send them out into the world, whichever sphere they are in. They need to learn how to operate in the power and authority of the Holy Spirit. This is something you may have to learn yourself. You may have to subject yourself to the Master so you may be taught by the Holy Spirit. Paul says, "This is how I do it, not with excellency of speech but with a demonstration of the Spirit's power" (See 1 Corinthians 2:4). The effectiveness of the gospel is in the demonstration of the Spirit's power, and we have not learned how to do that well. So, you need to take time out to learn how to do it, because you cannot give people what you don't have. This is key, and it is essentially important. You may have to lay hands and pray for a thousand people before you see your first miracle, but be persistent. The Disciples didn't get it right the first time either.

FINAL NOTE

I wrote this book to challenge us to dig deeper and not settle. Most of us are comfortable sitting in a building, waiting to die to go to heaven, but our lives have very little impact on those around us. Most of us don't engage in healing the sick, casting out demons, or raising the dead, yet this is seen as basic Christianity 101. We can cite a million reasons and doctrines to explain what happened, and why the church today is so different from what it was then, but truthfully, it doesn't even matter. What matters at this moment are the choices you make going forward.

The call for us is to "Come Up Higher," and it doesn't matter how high you go—there is always a higher place still. God is infinite, with unlimited power. No being anywhere is higher than God, and He has freely given us access to Himself, and one reason for that, I believe, is because of the mandate He has placed on our lives. There is much for us to do. The Christian Mystics of our day believe God rested on the seventh day because man was now present.

Take this call seriously. All creation is waiting on you.